About the author: For more than a decade, Blake Snow has written and published thousands of featured articles for half of the top twenty U.S. media, including *CNN*, *NBC*, *USA Today*, *Fox News*, *Wired Magazine*, and many other fancy publications and Fortune 500 companies. He lives in Provo, Utah, with his supportive family and loyal dog and is thrilled you picked this book. To learn more, please visit blakesnow.com.

LOG OFF

OFF

How to Stay Connected
after Disconnecting

BLAKE SNOW

Log Off: How to Stay Connected after Disconnecting /
by Blake Snow—Second printing: January 2018
ISBN: 9781973543749

Printed in the United States of America

For Lindsey... and the internet

Contents

Prologue: Why you should read this book

I wouldn't be what I am today without the internet: a work-from-home husband and father who enjoys greater flexibility than 99 percent of the rest of the world. Since discovering the internet as a teenager of the '90s, I have educated myself—both formally and informally—outfitted myself, informed myself, entertained myself, bettered myself, and employed myself with it.

In short, I owe the internet and its pioneers a lot. It changed my life and continues to do so, as does my iPhone, Kindle, or whatever latest and greatest whatchamacallit I'm late to adopt. (More on that later.)

At the same time, I refuse to spend my entire day online. In many ways, but not all ways, I view the internet as my cubicle. And why on earth would anyone want to live in a cubicle all day? Especially when there are better things to experience offline—the very things the online world can only simulate?

The answer seems obvious and yet, as the internet continues to play an increasing role in our lives, few have found it. And rather than being benefactors of connected devices like smartphones, we have attached to them at an alarming rate.

For example, 78 percent of those who have a mobile device admittedly stay "married to the office" while on vacation, according to a one survey. An equal number of smartphone users say they keep their device nearby while sleeping so they can hear when a new message arrives.

Relationships and marriages are being strained when one (or both) parties are more concerned with what's happening online than what's happening right in front of them, whether at the dinner table, for example, or during what should have been a romantic night on the town.

Worse still, breakfast is no longer the first stop in the morning, according to the *New York Times*. America, it seems, prefers a digital shot of emails, tweets, and wall updates over real-life eggs and hash browns—not unlike substance junkies.

Our generation even holds the pathetic distinction of rearing smartphone orphans, which is mind-numbingly ironic. The very devices that were meant to free us from the office to enjoy more time with family, peers, and children are, in fact, making us negligent lovers, friends, and parents.

In short, our wired lives are whack. Not just regular type, but wiggety whack. We have become zombies to modern technology. In fact, the *Oxford English Dictionary* defines "online" as being "controlled by or connected to a computer." That's no way to live.

As with all things in life, too much of anything is unhealthy. Except for maybe air guitar, chocolate cake, and dancing. But I digress. The trouble is: we've reached a point with personal technology that it is so accessible, so immediately gratifying, and so demanding that digital indulgence is no longer just affecting information junkies and borderline narcissists like myself. It's affecting everyone. If we don't stop to recalibrate our relationship with these powerful, life-changing, but also life-hindering, technologies, in just a few years we'll go from alarming habits to widespread burnout, debilitating attention spans, and universal digital anxiety disorder. We'll become slaves to the very devices that were meant to free us.

That's the reason I wrote this book. In addition to highlighting problematic consequences of our online behaviors, *Log Off: How to Stay Connected after Disconnecting* will document the personal lessons, reset advice, sagacious disciplines, and sustainable connectivity strategies I've learned and developed over the last decade.

Not only that, but I'll wax poetic on modern white-collar living, help you rediscover nights and weekends, and expel the wonders of low-caloric "internetting" and zero-calorie social media. I'll show you how to outperform a one-dimensional workaholic while keeping your sanity, how to recharge your battery in ways few have imagined, and why you might consider becoming a Reformed Luddite. In other words, I'll deliver what the title promises: how to stay connected after disconnecting.

If you're reading this, chances are you've felt out of control at some point with your relationship to email, the web, Facebook, messaging apps, Twitter, updates, YouTube, and smartphones, to name a few. And while I'm certainly not the first to endorse a balanced online lifestyle, I'm confident I'm one of the first to spell it out.

What you are about to read will not encourage you to write off technology on the whole, buy a year's supply of MREs, and take cover in the mountains. But it will teach you how to identify technology that works and technology that doesn't. What's more, it will help you take control of the more addicting distractions in your life, offer advice on rediscovering nights and weekends, explain post-online anxiety disorder, and provide sustainable strategies to living large on a low-caloric—but still capable of getting you ahead—technology diet.

Having lived for years on both sides of the track, I promise you the latter is indescribably better than the former. I hope your offline nirvana is as blissful as I know it can be.

Thanks for reading.

Chapter 1: Ending my affair with the virtual office

It all started in Montana.

For the first time in my adult life, I was exposed to the following harsh conditions while vacationing in Big Sky Country: no cell phone coverage and no internet access due to the picturesque cabin's remote location. My smartphone—which by then I had used for thirteen hundred consecutive days—was now useless. Out of its element.

As was I.

But instead of pouting about the circumstances, I was a good sport and embraced them. My family and I had secured lodging for the week with our closest friends (Hi, Andersens). The first national park in the world, Yellowstone, was fewer than five miles away. There were a pair of ATVs, a horseshoe pit, a canoe, a river within walking distance, and a tall, living-room-wide window overlooking a meadow and a moose lick. Plenty to do.

Besides, I thought to myself, I had worked for five straight years—through every previous vacation, in fact. I would enjoy a week off the grid then get back to the grind where I belonged.

Only that didn't happen. In that single week in Montana, I was shocked by how enriched my social life had suddenly become. As my wife noted after the trip, "With no online distractions, the entire party took on a completely different dynamic."

A better one, in fact. We were living in the present, in the moment, as they say, rather than having individual thoughts turned to what was happening elsewhere. We were seizing the day, smelling the roses, and all that crap for an entire week.

We conversed, observed nuances, and invented impromptu offline memes (just for us) as the week went on. Adults in attendance listened and engaged with one another instead of nodding insincerely or failing to acknowledge a thoughtful remark. Children had more access to their parents because the latter weren't distracted by grown-up stuff.

It was as if the world had stopped. But only because we as a group had inadvertently put the brakes on it. And our immediate lives were better because of it.

Upon returning home, I had a radical idea: Could I simulate and extend my "Montana Moment" indefinitely by canceling my smartphone's mobile internet? What would happen if I turned off all alerts and notifications on my phone (and computer), save for high-priority voice calls from those most important to me? Could I mentally leave the office at 5 p.m. each day, as I had already been doing physically? What other lifestyle habits could I cut back on, especially online ones, that could further enrich my offline life as an analog species living in an increasingly digital world?

For a wired geek like myself, these were not questions I considered lightly. I had told myself for years that subscribing to an always-on BlackBerry (remember those?) and later to an iPhone was helping me get ahead. I couldn't confirm it, but I *knew* I was making more money as a result. (With 20/20 hindsight, I wasn't.) I also told myself that, as a technology journalist, internet consultant, and someone who makes a living online, I just *had* to subscribe to every new piece of software and hardware to stay in the know. Simply put, I couldn't do my job, I told myself, unless I was completely immersed online.

What a load of bollocks, I soon discovered. Imagine if Henry Ford had stayed on the assembly line all day. We might still be driving slow and drafty, black Model Ts. Or imagine what kind of artificial stuff we'd be looking at if artists stayed cooped in their studios all day? Or the journalist who never left his desk to report from the field? Or the author who only ever read books instead of finding inspiration elsewhere before incorporating their experiences into their next best seller?

Those answers didn't come until after the jump, however. I'd never know for myself if I didn't try. So after a few months of going back and forth on the issue, I heard myself utter into a telephone what I thought I'd never say: "I'd like to cancel my mobile internet, please."

As a safety net, I verified with the perplexed customer service agent that I could resubscribe at any time without penalty.

Years later, I wouldn't dare return to my former internet habits. It's been that good. And please don't mistake me: I don't think data plans, mobile internet, or virtual offices are the devil. In fact, I think they're a great way to connect to the internet for someone who doesn't have access to it for much of their day at either work or home, as I do.

But they *are* the devil (or at least they can be) if *you* let them be. For me, they had become precisely that. I didn't have a little red devil sitting on my left shoulder. But staying connected at all hours of the day constantly distracted me with minutiae and low-priority (if not meaningless) stuff that was never going to change my life for the better. At best, it only helped me keep the status quo. I couldn't see big ideas (this book included) because I was myopic. I looked through the online looking glass without ever looking into the periphery.

Consequently, my personal life suffered. I no longer created music, a hobby I had loved as a teen. I didn't engage in sports or fitness like I used to. I couldn't carry on a conversation beyond "technology and business." And I was a dreadfully boring husband and borderline negligent father (more on that later).

In spite of all that, I abandoned my virtual office that day once and for all, as well as on nights and weekends. In return, I discovered that there are, in fact, enough hours in the day. You just have to admit that you'll never get everything done you want in a twenty-four-hour period. So why not put off whatever you were unable to accomplish after an honest day's work until the next working day or following Monday?

The mainstream answer is "because it gets you ahead," but it really doesn't. It just helps you spin your wheels in the mud. It provides the illusion of control and productivity.

For example, I used to idly sit at my desk for hours at a time "working" on a project. I would then worry endlessly while tied to my phone about how to get around the problem. Now I just say "screw it," walk away from work, go do something totally unrelated, then try again. I let my noodle and subconscious do the work behind the scenes. When combined, they almost always finish the job.

Admittedly, you don't have to reduce your online diet to make that decision, but the problem with always-on interneters is that they are more self-absorbed than most, and therefore unable to swallow the fact that the world will go on even in their absence (often for the better if they're not particularly inspired, which regularly happens to the serial distracted).

I only realized that when I cut loose entirely from the office on nights and weekends, save for no more than two to three emergencies per year. And I soon found out, I was returning to work more inspired, recharged, and focused than ever before.

I was basically telling my boss how it was going to be, sort of like that scene in *Fight Club* where Edward Norton goes crazy on his boss. Only I didn't beat myself up and extort a salary from my employer. I just recalibrated the boundaries of work moving forward.

Quitting my data plan wasn't the first time I had self-imposed rules to get a handle on my quality of life. In the last year of my data plan, when things became too much to bear at times, I'd purposely leave my nagging phone at home at night to enjoy leisure as much as I could. It didn't really work, however, as I dreaded coming home to all the things my phone had done while I was anxiously away. And what's the point of having such a convenient device if you couldn't use it, or worse, were worried by what it might introduce into your life at any given moment?

Simply put, before my "Montana Moment," (cheesy, I know—but catchy!) I was well on my way to burning out. As one of the lucky ones to make a career out of blogging before it became blasé, I was also one of the unlucky ones who used to read hundreds of comments in real time throughout the day on my tiny phone.

During that time, thanks to my enabling mobile internet, my brain was never really getting downtime. Put differently, imagine if you set your alarm clock every five minutes for an entire night, just to "check in" to make sure the house didn't burn down or any other non-issue you normally expect (or at least hope) not to go wrong. Then multiply that by four years. That's a lot of mental fatigue.

That's basically what we're doing to ourselves when "checking in" with our phones or online happenings at every other waking minute of the day. In addition to hopefully a good night's sleep, we already recognize the importance of physical downtime, or at least regular relaxation so our bodies can breathe. And yet we're not doing this with our minds—we're working them first thing in the morning until the last neuron has fired late in the night, or, in some cases, early the next morning.

For far too many of us, mental downtime is a thing of the past, and it's making us more distracted, more useless, and less productive than we've ever been.

And it's not just smartphones; it's every and any device that gives us its full, on-demand, "ask me any-thing you want, and I'll give you an immediate answer" attention—desktops, laptops, smartwatches, tablets, fitness trackers, and social media very much included.

The desktop web was, in fact, one of the first things that almost cost me my marriage. One year into my not-so-holy matrimony, I worked at home from eight in the morning until nine or ten at night—breaking only for a quick lunch and maybe an hour for dinner with the missus—before returning to my desk and all the glory the internet seemingly offered me.

On Saturdays, I would often put in four to eight additional hours, depending on my wife's demeanor. A year into this routine, my wife threw down the second gauntlet of our marriage (the first being to get me to commit to marrying her rather than postponing it for "a few years").

"Blake," she said sternly, "if we're going to live like this, let's go our separate ways. It's OK if this is how you want to live your life—working the majority of it—but it's not how I want to live mine, so maybe we should split."

She wasn't bluffing. I imagine I said something cliché like, "I'm trying to provide a future for our family," but she was right. What's the point in settling down if we didn't "settle down." Long story short, she got me to commit to leaving the office by 6 p.m. at the latest, not unlike the hour "Beaver" Cleaver's dad fictitiously ar-rived home.

Little did my wife know, I would begin the all-day affair with my office again one year later, thanks to the help of my inconspicuous and easier-to-hide (since it fit in my pocket) smartphone.

I'll fill in the gaps as we move along with the story. Suffice it to say, I've enjoyed many exciting vacations in my life. But that week in Montana is special to me. More than just a getaway, it was a life-changing moment and the primary catalyst for the subsequent balance, focus, and even accomplishments that would follow.

Chapter 2: Why the internet is hard to put down

The "king complex." That's the reason it's difficult for many individuals to leave the internet—even for as little as a few hours in the evening, over a weekend, or on vacation. In short, the internet makes us feel like kings. It is the ultimate concierge.

"Bring me this," I demand, and it does. "More!" I say. It complies. "Still more!" It does not disappoint. "Let me watch, this, that, and the other." Each time, I ask, it delivers, because it's endless. When I run out of requests, I move to new subjects and interests.

To meet our demands, the internet must always listen to us. It gives us its undivided attention. Unlike humans, the internet never fails to recognize our presence, our thoughts, or our input. It is always there. It never leaves the room. It never takes vacation. It never fails in making us feel like we have a full-time personal assistant, if not a cadre of them.

But since the internet cannot empathize with us, we need it to talk back. It does that, too, with countless links, search results, and even spoken replies now. In worst-case scenarios, it at least has the courtesy to say something like "cannot compute" or "Zero results. Did you mean this, that, or the other?" And so we ask it something else.

In the event the internet is unable to supply what we ask of it—say, a physical experience, creation, or sensation—it will simulate that experience as often as we like from all possible angles: videos, photos, second-hand observations and reviews by those who have actually experienced what we're after. Some would say it's even better than the real thing.

In other words, the internet offers power, or at least the illusion of it. That's the real reason the internet is so addicting. For the first time in human history, mere serfs can convincingly simulate the experience of kings and exercise dominion over digital domains—their own fantasized corner of reality. On the internet. With a sea of subjects.

Hence, the internet gets abused, more by some than others—readers of this book likely included. But it's not the internet's fault. It's ours. As with all things in life, humans abuse power. The internet just happens to be the latest and greatest abuse of power, at least for the masses.

In addition to making us feel powerful, the internet tickles our need for socialization. Although it fails to recreate human touch, physical presence, live emotion, or free-flowing conversation, the internet is better than the alternative, even if it can only provide a colder, diluted, less meaningful, or synthetic form of socialization.

For instance, I tell it, "Show me how many people I know, and make me feel like I'm involved in their lives." Thanks to social media such as Facebook, Instagram, and other networking tools, the internet can do that now, too.

Obviously, there are lots of live humans to interact with on the internet. But we usually only get to interact with the remnants of one, e.g., a typed artifact left long ago, such as an old email or an even older online comment. While online, we really only interact with traces of humans, often at the expense of real-time correspondence.

Instant messaging and online gaming are obvious exceptions. But even those fail to convey nonverbal language, which accounts for more than 70 percent of communication, by most accounts. Never mind that instant messaging and online gamers account for only a fraction of total internet users.

Consequently, the vast majority of one's online time is spent in isolation—well more than 90 percent by some estimates.

For online kings, it's lonely at the top. But unlike real-world kings, online ones don't necessarily sacrifice relationships by burning bridges. We willingly neglect them.

How could this be? We are social creatures, after all. Why would someone willingly subject themselves to loneliness, isolation, and stale social interactions in pursuit of virtual reality?

Science has the answer. It comes in two parts. The first is dopamine, a rewarding chemical the brain releases that causes us to want, desire, and seek out favorable experiences. Previously thought to be the cause of pleasure, "Dopamine actually makes us curious about ideas and fuels our search for information," I was told by Dr. Susan Weinschenk, a respected behavioral scientist.

From an evolutionary standpoint, that's a good thing. "Seeking is more likely to keep us alive than sitting around in a satisfied stupor," adds Weinschenk. But under the distorted conditions that we now live, dopamine becomes a problem. One internet artist cleverly visualized this with *The Evolution of Computer Man* (Google it), which depicts a slouched chimpanzee evolving into a lurching ape, a tool-using and upright Neanderthal, and ultimately a Homo Sapien hunched over a desktop keyboard or smartphone.

Which brings us to the second part of the answer: cheap, instant, and near-limitless gratification, which perfectly describes the internet. Under those rare and revolutionary conditions, an estimated 15 percent of people (and growing) get stuck in an endless dopamine loop.

Remember that time you went online in search of a simple answer, only to find yourself, two hours later, clicking on links that had nothing to do with the original answer you sought? That's a dopamine loop. It's the scientific reason we end up online more than we plan to. It explains why we can't put our smartphones down. It explains why some people neglect real life in favor of virtual life. And it leads to compulsive disorders, similar to those who are addicted to chemical stimulants and depressants such as cocaine, caffeine, methamphetamines, nicotine, and alcohol.

"Dopamine starts us seeking, then we get rewarded for the seeking, which makes us seek more," explains Weinschenk. "It becomes harder and harder to stop looking at email, texts, web links, or our smartphones to see if we have a new message or alert."

Worst still, research shows the dopamine system is bottomless. Since it doesn't have satiation built in, dopamine keeps demanding "more, more, more!" And it goes absolutely bonkers when unpredictability is introduced—say, an unexpected email, text, or app alert from who knows what and who knows whom. Surprise! It's just like Pavlov's famous and classically conditioned dogs, for those who remember your introductory college psychology course.

"It's the same system at work for gambling and slot machines," explains Weinschenk. "Since dopamine is involved in variable reinforcement schedules, it's especially sensitive to dings, visual alerts, or any other cue that a reward is coming, which sends our dopamine system raging."

And so we stay online and on our phones longer than anticipated. We forgo our offline lives. It's science.

But it's mostly power. History proves this.

You see, many of the world's most powerful individuals have died alone. Their pursuit of power usually comes at the expense of unpaid relationships. At the end of life, they predictably find themselves surrounded by no one, wishing they had spent less time working (the number two regret of the dying, according to Bronnie Ware's excellent research) and more time developing relationships (number three on her list).

And so it is with our online lives. Yes, the internet *simulates* friendship, community, and conversation better than anything the world has ever seen. But it's no substitute for the real thing.

In fact, no evidence suggests that Facebook, Twitter, and other so-called "social" media have actually increased the number of social interactions taking place offline (at least unpaid ones).

The same is true of the entire internet. It's a phenomenal resource—the penicillin of my generation, the linchpin of the information age, if not something more.

But we've abused it. We've corrupted it. And we've gotten big-headed as a result. "I was a winner online, but a loser offline," one recovering user recently confessed to me.

Although more "connected" than ever before now, we're also more detached than ever before—all because of the king complex that many of us wrestle with everyday.

It's time we kill the king.

Chapter 3: Off with his head!

Because I'm a borderline narcissist, I required extreme measures to overthrow my king. Before mobile internet was commonplace, many working professionals paid extra for the privilege. For many years, I was one of them. Until my "Montana Moment," that is. After that enlightening week, I canceled my data plan with the understanding that I could always re-up if the separation anxiety became too much to bear.

This was undoubtedly a first-world problem—I get it. But for someone who had previously spent every single day attached to a smartphone from waking up until sleep, it mattered. So, after four "always-on" years of faithfully paying for mobile internet and effectively imposing an inescapable work leash upon myself, I cut it. Unexpectedly, the following half decade was one of the most productive and invigorating ones of my career.

Without the omnipresent distraction of "elsewhere" on my phone, my income and, more importantly, my relationships increased dramatically year over year. My resulting tax returns, relationships with immediate family, and face-to-face encounters are living proof of that increase.

Up to that point, I had wrongly assumed that the longer I stayed online, the more I would be contributing to the world and helping my bottom line. What a crock. For the majority of my twenties and into my early thirties, I was working quantitatively, not qualitatively. I was stuck in neutral instead of taking rejuvenating breaks every ninety minutes or so, which are proven to refresh our minds and let our subconscious do the heavy lifting.

Not to mention, I wasn't "batching" (or batch processing) everyday tasks, which led to a lot of wasted time, energy, focus, and ideas (more on that in chapter 6).

Obviously, we each have our own challenges, but I'm not the only one. Over the years, I've encountered significant amounts of people who struggle with similar problems. That being the case, I believe we must each kill our own tyrannical kings. Or at least limit his power if we hope to master our offline domain and live for now.

How can this be done? While I can't speak for everyone, here are ten changes I made in my life to overthrow and exile the king for the past eight years:

1. **Cut the cord.** I quit my affair with the internet "cold turkey," similar to how I quit a nasty habit of smoking after throwing a near-full pack of Marlboro Lights from a moving car in 1998. (Sorry, environment.) Although drastic, this measure was exactly what I, my inner king (and, previously, my lungs) needed to recalibrate my values. In my case, I removed the temptation by canceling my mobile internet plan. Others have found success in using website or app blockers or deleting addicting apps from their phone altogether. Whatever you choose, you need to stay clear from temptation to give your mind a chance to experience life without pervasive internet.

2. **Establish an accountability partner.** That is someone you can confide in and account to with your stated desire to scale back your internetting. Inform your friends and family that you are going to quit and ask for their encouragement. In my case, I enlisted the supervision of my wife. I told her what I wanted to do and asked her to keep me honest. It worked. As with all addictions, this step is arguably the most empowering. We're social creatures, after all. Use that to your advantage.

3. **Replace bad habits with new distractions.** Preferably, obtain outdoor ones—something that can remind you of, if not rekindle, the joy of physiological experiences as opposed to virtual, simulated, or mental-only ones. Like many people, I took up hiking, travel, and fitness as ways to experience the brave new analog world in my life. I reduced the number of video games and other "screen stimulants" I had grown accustomed to. Not because they were bad, but because they didn't mesh well with my new lifestyle. While breaking up with this things, I basically told them, "It's me, not you."

4. **Change your routine.** If you always use the internet at certain times of the day or in a certain environment or with a certain group of friends, take a break from them. Avoid activities related to fully engrossed internetting until your "withdrawal symptoms" subside. I lifted that line directly from substance abuse counsel. Although compulsive internet disorder isn't technically a psychiatric disorder, it is very real and requires similar measures to overcome. In my case, I canceled mobile data and limited the amount of time I spent on my still-connected desktop. I did this mainly with the help of number three above and the following:

5. **Be active.** Because we've created such a convenient lifestyle for ourselves, at least in first-world countries (e.g., free two-day shipping on mail-order anything), it's easy to forget what analog experiences feel like— at least exciting, non-routine, or otherwise demanding ones. That's where an exercise regimen comes in. More than anything, this habit can distract your mind (and king) from what's going on elsewhere to what's going on right now. Namely, "Keep breathing!" or "Why do my muscles burn so much?" To make fitness and movement a new habit in your life, however, you must find a better motivator than weight. In my case, it was realizing that I'll probably never leave my dependents with a lot of money or notoriety upon my death. So I threw away my scale, used my jeans as feedback, and gave my family the next best thing: the long-term commitment of being there for them as long as I possibly can with the life-giving and heart-strengthening help of regular exercise.

6. **Become a late adopter.** Staying up-to-date with the latest and greatest news, technology, products, fashion, celebrity gossip, episodic content, and even social trends is a fool's errand. Not only does it allow other people's thinking to dictate what you value, it suggests when and how you should value things that might have little to no effect on your daily fulfillment. Furthermore, this behavior also fuels excessive internetting, which is the greatest tool ever invented to stay up-to-date. But it's also an illusion. If you don't know what's important, it doesn't matter how fast you stay up-to-date in life. So become a late adopter. Before letting something into your life, ask yourself, "Do I need this, or will it make my life significantly better?" If no, don't adopt it! The more you do this, the more free time you'll establish in your daily routine to fill it with things, people, and experiences that truly matter. That's what I call living large on low-caloric technology.

7. **Find balance in thirds.** Some life coaches or productivity gurus argue that you cannot find balance in life. I wholeheartedly disagree. While there are certainly seasons in life that require concentrated attention in one area of life over another, or when ongoing emergencies persist, I believe we all can and should strive for balance in three key areas: sleep time, work time (including professional, volunteer, domestic maintenance, and personal errands), and free time (i.e., leisure, relaxation, hobbies, movies, music, games, chasing curiosities, self-reflection, and thought-provoking activities such as reading). Ideally, customarily, and even scientifically (according to most studies on the subject of ideal productivity times), this should be done in three groups of eight hours each per day. They don't have to be blocked off or perfectly timed, obviously. For instance, you may be required to work overtime or pay special attention to house maintenance one day, then you will try to balance that cost elsewhere on another day or over the weekend. Note: many people are tempted to work more by cutting into both sleep and free time in their early to middle ages, only to find that this lessens their longevity and life expectancy. In other words, many people have tried, but no one has beaten the sands of time, at least not yet. Best to stick to the Rule Of Thirds (more on this in chapter 8).

8. **Periodically fast from electronics.** My wife and children are not fans of this, but electronic fasts have served our family well over the past several years. They work like this: pick an entire week—we do one in spring and one in fall—in which you turn off and avoid all electronic devices (save for living utilities). That means no iPhones, computers, Kindles, tablets, TV, video games, or any other electronic diversions. Doing this jolts your memory and forces you to get creative in how you spend your free and personal time. Think of it as an electronic oil change twice a year.

9. **Devote yourself to weekly creative hours.** Confession: it took me nearly a decade to complete this book. I wrote the first quarter in early 2009 shortly after conceiving it. Then fear and writer's block happened. Then I wrote another 10 percent a few years later. Then fear and writer's block set in again. Finally, I finished the remaining two-thirds in one autumn month in 2017—almost eight years later. What changed? A client of mine and two-time author recommended weekly creative hours. Similar to electronic fasts, no consumption, assigned work, or socialization is allowed during creative hours. Rather, you must voluntarily create something. During these hours, my wife has made bracelets, written in her journal, or colored in stress-relieving adult coloring books. My children colored, produced arts and crafts, or fastened trinkets to sell alongside lemonade stands. I began using that time to finish this book. Although one hour a week doesn't seem like much, it was enough to build momentum to one very productive month of writing. And here we are.

10. **Rediscover nights and weekends.** Admittedly, this is more of a lifestyle choice and incorporates much of the above. But I can tell you that after first experiencing this in the pre-web and limited-information era, then losing it during my aspirational twenties, and then finding it again in my early thirties, how sweet this part of life can be. Depending on how you spend your weekdays, this is where a large swath of free time, subconscious thought, devoted hobbies, self-reflection, and worship can and should take place after a busy, demanding, or otherwise stressful workweek. It's how you let your mind and body recharge before the coming week. On weeknights and weekends, we can leverage sizable chunks of free time to accomplish something we've always wanted to do and prepare for the next chapter (or job) in our life. Either way, it is in these moments that most of us can reflect upon the meaning we find in all waking or conscious

moments of our lives.

When deciding how to overthrow your king, you'll undoubtedly encounter separation anxiety. I know I did. The trick is replacing the king's absence with something new and hopefully exciting so you don't resort to mindlessly scanning your phone or staring into a glowing "fun" box in search of trivial dopamine loops for hours on end—a default and popular act that will never take you anywhere.

I'm convinced that mobile internet will someday replace the residential broadband cable or fiber lines many of us use to access the internet today. For workers, employees, entrepreneurs, extended-stay vacationers, or anyone who doesn't have access to the internet at work or home, mobile internet is undeniably a net gain for humanity. This tool is not the problem. But many of us certainly are when armed with mobile internet. To free ourselves from their alluring, bottomless, and magical properties, we must redraw the boundary lines between us and them. We cannot do this while suffering from myopia. We have to distance ourselves from them in order to redefine our relationship with them.

A note on digital detox clinics: If you have to pay someone a lot of money to temporarily solve your problem, you're probably not going to be able to do it alone later, which is what you'll need to do if you want sustainable, life-changing results. While "digital detoxing" is certainly well-intentioned, it's also similar to fad dieting (i.e., very poor odds of long-term success). Ultimately, you'll need to institute everyday changes to your lifestyle and habits if you wish to improve your long-term prospects.

Chapter 4: Ooh la la! How my online affair started

My obsession with on-demand information began when I was four feet tall. As a university administrator in the early '90s, my father was part of a minority of Americans with early access to the internet. Mind you, this was before dial-up home internet went mainstream in the mid-nineties.

One evening, my dad asked if I wanted to accompany him to his office. His job didn't require much computer work then, so I had free reign with the "magic box" while Dad did what the ancients used to call "paperwork" on his mahogany desk.

I went for the Macintosh, admittedly, but stayed for the Yahoo. Specifically, I stayed for the internet. If you'll remember, Yahoo was the most popular "portal," or internet directory, at the time. Before Google, searching was futile. The best way to shimmy around the internet was clicking on a topical guide of links provided by Yahoo, Lycos, MSN, or one of the many other bygone portals. Either way, it was good times for curious minds.

After discovering this electronic encyclopedia of wonderful things—including everything a thirteen-year-old boy could imagine—I started asking my dad to work late just so I could futz around on the internet. "Are you going to your office later tonight?" I'd ask. Sometimes he obliged even though it was obvious he didn't have much to do. I think he liked that I took such an interest.

Truth be told, I was using him—Yahoo beckoned. In fact, I'd drop just about anything for a chance to stay current with the internet. Instead of yakking on the phone at night with classmates, I'd check in with a pen pal from England in something called a "chat room." Hot stuff back then.

Instead of playing hooky off campus with friends during high school, I'd often skip class for the humble "internet Lab," which consisted of just four desktop computers. It doesn't sound like much, but even that was oversupply. I don't ever recall seeing another adolescent soul beside me. Either that, or I was too engrossed with endless links to even notice. (Fun fact: The more popular computers in the '90s stayed offline and were dubbed "multimedia" computers capable of playing games and CD-ROMS—also hot stuff back then.)

Print was dying before my very eyes—a net gain, to be sure—and no one seemed to care. Instead of waiting for updates to be broadcasted or delivered to me at a later time, I could summon the internet to bring me the latest and greatest immediately. It made for some of the best education my high school ever gave me.

In college, my peers went from zero interest in the internet to that of passing interest. For them, it was seemingly more of a novelty medium than the revolutionary one I believed it to be. At a mid-range university of no more than fifteen thousand students, the Internet Lab went from four occupants in high school to maybe sixteen in college.

That was in 2001. Today, many universities make thousands of internet-connected desktops, laptops, and other devices available to students.

In any case, I had formed a special bond to the on-demand information of the internet during that Jurassic era of collegiate connectivity.

But it didn't become cruel love until after graduating from college and getting married, as mentioned previously. It didn't reach secret-combination status until after I acquired my first laptop. And it didn't reach epidemic proportions until purchasing my first smartphone in January of 2006—a thick, blue, pebble-looking thing called "BlackBerry."

Although desktop internet had me at "Hello," I was able to tame and remove myself from it with a little bit of discipline and tough love from my better half. When I discovered mobile internet, however, my attraction became fatal.

I am not alone in this. Rather than being patrons of smartphones, much of society has become slaves to them at an alarming rate. Remember the previously shared stats: three quarters of smartphone owners keep their phone nearby while sleeping so they can hear new messages arrive and a similar number admit to working while on vacation.

In addition, more than 30 percent of smartphone users admit to feeling "married to the office" at all times, according to a recent Aol survey. One in ten say they are "addicted" to their smartphone. How lovely.

Don't worry. It gets worse. The way we use our smartphones compounds the problem. Twenty years ago, about 70 percent of Americans wore watches to keep time. Today, that number is less than 30 percent because most of our phones double as watches. That wasn't such a big deal with dumbphones because they didn't distract us after checking the time.

With smartphones, however, an estimated 85 percent of owners "constantly" check their flat-screen pocket watches for time. When they do, users get distracted by new alerts, invitations, and notifications, something plain ol' wristwatches are incapable of. (Pro-tip: When you're ready to reign in your smartphone use, you'll need to get a wristwatch *stat*. And not a smartwatch that talks with your phone—a dumb one that just tells time.)

The relationship with our phones has gotten so bad, many of us suffer anxiety attacks when stuck without them. "For some, not having their phone raises their heart rate," reported one therapist. "These panic attacks are almost identical to alcohol, gambling, food or drug addiction."

Of course, the American Medical Association doesn't classify excessive internet or smartphone abuse as an addictions. Like any other general compulsion disorder, they're classified as such. But that hasn't stopped a significant number of smartphone users from seeking professional help. In fact, a 2013 survey found that more than 10 percent of smartphone users have been treated by a growing number of internet therapists. And that number has reportedly risen every year since.

But the real kicker is this: smartphones have made our lives worse in more ways than one. A Stanford University study recently found that as internet and smartphone use grows, "Americans report they spend less time with friends and family, shopping in stores, or watching television, and more time working for their employers at home—without cutting back their hours in the office."

As a result, love interests, children (or, sometimes, "digital orphans"), friendships, and even dogs are neglected. Although billed as "social networking," this technology often fragments and separates us. It certainly doesn't always increase the number of face-to-face social engagements we enjoy offline.

No, modern society is best summed up by this: alone together.

What a depressing reality from technology that holds so much promise. When used properly, smartphones are capable of helping us work, live, learn, do, and play more effectively. Having the internet in your pocket, your work desk, or home can be a wonderful convenience. Such access has changed our lives forever, sometimes for the better.

But more often than not, many of us abuse this power. Even after extended periods of detox.

I'm a prime example of this. A few years after canceling mobile internet, my carrier added it back for free. *Turn-by-turn navigation will be nice,* I immediately and confidently thought to myself. But even though I had largely mastered a healthy relationship with my phone in the preceding years with self-imposed limits, the constant allure of the internet, anytime updates, and emails are nearly as strong today as when I first quit.

Because I'm human, I still have to fight urges. I still have to ask myself, *Blake, do you really want to open this message and all the work-related baggage and mental focus that come with it? Do you really want to leave the place you're in right now to someplace that isn't going anywhere?*

Of course, you'll have to answer a lot more questions than that to stay strong. I'll get to those later. But by understanding how your fling with the internet, your smartphone, or [insert other digital obsession or app here] started, you'll better understand your needs and wants and how best to tame them to achieve your ideal offline lifestyle.

Chapter 5: Why real life is better

There's very little, if any, doubt: social media obsessions increase feelings of loneliness and alienation while decreasing gratitude and ultimate satisfaction. In the decade that I've researched and closely followed the rise and consequences of social media abuse, I've yet to encounter any evidence suggesting otherwise. In fact, new research underscores the damaging behavior.

"Exposure to the carefully curated images from others' lives leads to negative self-comparison," concluded a recent study from Harvard University, a.k.a. the birthplace of Facebook. "The sheer quantity of social media interaction may detract from more meaningful real-life experiences." In other words, the more you use social media such as Facebook, Twitter, Instagram, or whatever eventually supplements or replaces them, the worse you feel.

The reason: social media is largely an illusion and rarely an enhancement. Like an artificial sweetener, it might lead us to believe that we have a large and thriving social circle and support group, but ultimately it fails to satiate our social needs. Increasing our number of *electronic* friends does not—for the most part—meet our emotional, intimate, in-person, affectionate, and... ahem, social needs. Since many users edit, manipulate, manufacture, and revise the most flattering highlights of their lives, we may be tempted to compare the seemingly everyday highlights of others with our personal lowlights. Not only does this occurrence make us feel inadequate, but it also disables our ability to gain a true understanding of who people really are.

Before I write another word, let the record show that I admire Mark Zuckerberg, the creator of Facebook. I think his world-changing platform has done much good and does indeed offer support to those in need, especially the elderly, the disabled, and anyone else with special or peculiar social needs. Although I'm no longer a user, I'm confident it's helped millions of people. Hence my hesitancy to wholeheartedly vilify it or any other digital "place for friends."

That said, I'm not sure if Facebook and other social software have been a net gain to modern society, at least when compared to their contemporaries such as Google search, microprocessors, or email. The social network is undoubtedly a powerful tool. To be clear, its abusers—not the tool itself—shoulder the blame. But I worry that the majority of people are largely incapable of moderating themselves to healthy, uplifting, and enriching use of it.

For example, my wife was recently updated by a friend on the latter's recent announcements and developments. Since my wife no longer subscribes to universal social media (only private ad-hoc groups such as Hangouts or GroupMe as needed), she largely remains out of the loop when talking with friends and family until she speaks with them directly, either in-person, via text message, or over the phone. Because of that, the encounter was much more rewarding, according to her friend. "It's so nice to be able to talk to you in greater detail than with other friends who only passingly saw a picture or read a couple of sentences about what I've done," the friend said.

I experienced the same realization many years ago after quietly quitting Facebook. At the time, I feared I might be committing social suicide. Today, I can happily report that didn't happen.

Since quitting the popular watering hole, I've limited the number of professional and personal distractions I encounter on a near minute-to-minute basis. I no longer suffer from "fear of missing out" (FOMO) syndrome, nor do I feel the desire to "check in" every waking hour. Granted, it might take me a few more days than most to stay current on the latest trends. The daily threat of falling sky has dissipated. And I certainly can't tell you what my friends had for lunch yesterday.

But I also don't have to consciously decide or waste mental resources on distinguishing friends from colleagues, associates, and nobodies. Now I just let my relationships happen naturally: unannounced and constantly evolving.

Since quitting, I do miss the little updates from those dearest to me. I'm incredibly out of date and out of touch with my cousins, aunts, uncles, and friends I hope to encounter again. But this hasn't affected my happiness and everyday social satisfaction. The trade-off has been worth it, especially since those closest to me naturally keep me up-to-date on the really important, newsworthy stuff happening to extended family, friends, community, and larger world.

Another important lesson learned: I still get invited to parties and events, at least by those who really want me there. And I'm more motivated to reach out and see people in person since I don't encounter them online as much as I used to.

The biggest thing I've learned since quitting Facebook, however, is this: whether online or off, the cream of life always rises to the top. The best status updates always transcend mediums—the internet very much included.

Admittedly, this is a hard lesson to learn that requires patience. As a parent, it's equally hard to teach. For instance, my ten-year-old is especially interested in becoming famous. She enjoys watching YouTube "vloggers," a.k.a. everyday individuals talking into the camera while living seemingly extraordinary and glamorous lives. She also enjoys music.

In those two interests, she is not alone; so much so that there is now popular music software that lets aspirational users like my daughter share their own music videos with others, count how many people like and view the video, and ultimately gain followers (and hopefully fame), much like vloggers.

Upon discovering this "app," my daughter took an immediate and obsessive interest. Instead of pursuing personal passions as she had before—such as art and playing with neighborhood friends outside—she spent most of her free time isolated in her room. Of course, this behavior was negatively affecting her demeanor. She was sullen, emotionless, and distant rather than bright, smiling, and playful like before.

After several months of this, my wife eventually expressed her concern and one day announced to my daughter that the app was no longer allowed. "I was mad and sad about this because *all of my friends* were on it," my daughter later wrote in a journal entry (emphasis mine) that she shared with her mother and I. "I started to become addicted and started to feel jealousy towards other people on the app." She also mentioned feeling inadequate about her legs when compared to other pairs seen on the app.

To be clear, compulsive behaviors, jealousy, and unfair comparisons existed long before this app, my daughter, social media, or even electricity existed. But for a ten-year-old, developing girl, it certainly expedited, if not prematurely exposed her to, these feelings. In the ensuing months after deleting the app, our daughter returned to normal: carefree, confident, innocent, joyful.

A year after deleting my Facebook account, I wrote a special report for *CNN* on "Why some dissatisfied users are quitting Facebook." Unsurprisingly, Facebook officials told me their service is good for humanity. Surprisingly, they likened the service to eating your vegetables. "Facebook can be like broccoli," one representative told me at the time. "Everyone can benefit from it but not everyone will want to. If you have a good experience, we hope you'll stay. If not, come back and see us again, because we're constantly working to delight people in ways that aren't possible offline."

Let's acknowledge some of those "delightful" features that aren't possible offline. Consider a favorite of mine: animated GIFs, pronounced with a hard "g" because "Jif" is peanut butter. With those delightful things —GIFs, not peanut butter—I can speak in gestures and convey meaning without ever using words. I can express a range of emotion not humanly possible before. I can do a little of that offline. But not nearly as much as I can online.

Aaaaaand that's about it. What's more, you don't need to subscribe to one social network over another to take advantage of GIFs or other online conveniences.

But those are sidenotes to a much larger social story. This story is this: much of life will be spent alone —even for those in a relationship or with children—and that's OK. Finding joy in mundane experiences such as washing dishes is not only OK, it's healthy. The problem with social media is that it often undermines both of those truths, or seemingly creates the false perception that neither exists in a self-promoted world where only the sexy things get broadcasted and shared—as if normal levels of loneliness and monotony are somehow bad.

All told, "Social media has complicated the meaning of friend," says my lifelong, in-person, and loyal friend Josh Rhine. Moreover, many people use social media as a shortcut for the more time-consuming and meaningful relationships taking place offline.

What's the fix? For many (if not most) users, the answer, again, is, "Off with his head!" We must kill the king. This is especially true for full-blown or moderate narcissists like myself, which one study by *Psychology Today* pegged at a whopping 30 percent of young people, more than double last generation's numbers.

The more specific answer is that private social groups such as Hangouts, GroupMe, or simple group texts are more functional and less detrimental than widespread and public platforms such as Facebook, Instagram, and Twitter. Even in cases of the former, however, you must ask yourself: Is what I'm doing strengthening my relationships and prospects or distracting me from doing both?

To any who feel that deleting their favorite social network or "time-suck of the month" would somehow hinder their social and professional prospects, the burden of proof is on them. Having found online nirvana almost eight years ago after quitting mainstream social media, my social and professional prospects significantly grew. I still meet people face-to-face—more so now than before. I still have a phone. I still use email. I still use temporary private networks, calendar invites, and group messaging as needed to stay connected with, augment, and deepen my relationships with offline friends, family, and colleagues. And I use those same tools to foster new online relationships.

But, in my experience, online relationships are far less successful than the face-to-face ones I naturally foster offline while rubbing elbows with fresh people in new, and sometimes even old, places.

Chapter 6: How excessive internetting kills our spirit

Power corrupts. That's the best way to describe the cumulative effect that take-anywhere smartphones have on us. It's not their fault. Power alone can't be blamed. But the abuse of it can. The burden is ours.

Even mild internet users who have quit or otherwise reduced their digital consumption struggle. Just recently, my wife turned to me and said, "I'm going to take a break from my phone." This came from someone who doesn't participate in any mainstream social media platforms—only a small group of twenty family members and a couple of compelling games.

"I didn't notice a problem," I replied.

Like most abusers of smartphones (read: all of us), my wife had gotten really good at hiding her affair. "I didn't like how I was getting anxious whenever I was without my phone," she said. "So I'm making a concerted effort to leave it behind when I know it's not needed or may become a distraction to the moment."

I applauded her efforts, but I also had an intimidating thought: If disciplined people with fortified boundaries like my wife struggle to overcome the pull of a smartphone, what chance do the rest of us have?

The answer is discouragingly complicated. But it can be found, especially when we move beyond willpower alone and start implementing disciplined, calculated, and ultimately tempered use of these power-fully informative, communicative, and endlessly enter-taining tools. (More on that in the next chapter.) For now, I'd like to focus on how excessive online use kills our individual, and even collective, spirits.

First, excessive internetting makes us negligent drivers, lovers, friends, and even parents. Several years ago, I laid my baby daughter on our living room ottoman to kick and play. She was only a few months old. Her two-and-a-half-year-old sister merrily played nearby. With the coast clear, I decided to work on my laptop-fathering skills. I was head down, staring into an electric screen, entrenched in technology.

Moments later, my eldest shouted, "Maddie's fall-ing!" I heard a heavy thud, then brief silence as some-one's lungs slowly recovered after having the wind knocked out of them. And then I heard a burst of crying.

I looked up from my PowerBook (remember those?), only to find a suspicious-looking toddler (Sadie) standing over a fallen baby (Maddie), who was still cry-ing loudly. I dashed to the latter's rescue, ensured she was OK, and then proceeded to discipline Sadie in anger, who I believed had deliberately sabotaged her younger sibling. "Don't do that again," I sternly told the suspected perpetrator, as I replaced the now-quieted baby on the ottoman again. I then returned to who-knows-what on the computer.

A short while later, I heard an innocent voice cry out again, "Maddie's falling!" This time, however, the voice came from afar. I looked up to find a bashful little blonde girl in the corner of the room, pointing to the baby, who was teetering on the edge of the ottoman. I sprung from the sofa and caught her before falling a second time.

Immediately, I realized what I had foolishly done.

"You didn't pull your sister from the ottoman, did you?" I asked the upright child in the corner of the room.

"No, Daddy," she replied, looking much like the big-eyed, adorable, and acceptance-seeking orange tabby cat that famously starred in Shrek 2.

Unbeknownst to me, child number two had learned to shimmy herself off the ottoman since I had last watched her. (They really do grow up so fast!) My eldest wasn't being vindictive, it turns out. She was simply trying to alert an absent parent. And she was smart enough to do it from a distance the second time for fear I would pounce again if I found her near the scene of the accident.

I felt rotten and discouraged as a young father. All because of fleeting digital stuff I had since forgotten but taken such a strong interest in that morning.

Here's another, more pertinent example of how excessive internetting kills our spirit. Google, Facebook, Microsoft, and other economic behemoths hire some of the brightest minds and mathematicians in the world. These are the most sought-after private employers and some of the biggest recruiters of scientists around.

What do most of these hired eggheads work on, you ask? How to get you and me to click on more online ads. Really. They work with advanced algorithms, behavioral science, and complex calculations to "optimize" the amount of time we spend clicking and consuming "just one more link." The more we click, the more money they garner.

It's gotten so bad, in fact—or good, depending on whose side you're on—that some of our brightest minds get lured into doing basic tech support at high-earning brands or conducting color psychology experiments to see which hue gets people to click more. It's draining our talent and preventing masterminds from solving truly bigger issues such as continued water, energy, economic, and sanitation scarcity. Talk about unintended consequences.

In exchange, these crackpots get the best salaries, free meals, dry cleaning, extended leaves of absence, and childcare. They also work in environments that would make Tom Hank's character in Big blush, not to mention quadruple the amount of vacation time. Those kinds of perks alone are enough to sidetrack some of our brightest minds—because money talks.

Don't misunderstand me. I'm a practicing and ardent capitalist. It's a free world. The above companies and the people they employ can do whatever they like. I respect their ability to choose. And I don't think that mainstream tech or otherwise online companies are inherently evil by any means. In fact, I quite like them and regularly trust my online searches and privacy to their care.

Truth be told, they're just supplying what the market demands: more free internet, information, and virtual distractions—all made possible by ads.

The downside, however, is that the internet and all its forms have become digital "Soma" for many users. Instead of willingly submitting ourselves to a numbed mental state with futuristic substances—as Aldous Huxley eerily predicted we would in Brave New World using a drug called Soma—we're willingly doing it with digital diversions and online leisure.

These companies aren't entirely innocent, of course. But neither are we. We're just as indifferent toward the human condition as they are. We're willingly neglecting and consequently killing our collective spirit.

Still not convinced? Here's another example: multitasking. That first became a word in the 1960s when researchers began studying its negative effect on human productivity, efficiency, and accuracy. But until the birth of the web and, ultimately, the internet, that's always in our pockets now, multitasking remained on the fringes of society. Now it kills people driving on roads, all because of the internet's ability to make us think and feel superhuman in terms of what we're capable of accomplishing. Again, power corrupts.

In truth, numerous studies, scientific literature, academic papers, media reports, and even business research all stress the fact that multitasking of any kind reduces productivity and increases human error. Many more show that online multitasking is a mythical pipe dream—one that worsens our memory, frustrates relationships, slows us down, stresses us out, blinds us from our immediate (and often pleasant) surroundings, causes overeating, and dampens creativity.

Excessive internetting has only exacerbated this behavior, if not introduced it into the mainstream. Estimated annual losses stemming from multitasking are fast approaching $1 trillion per year in the United States alone, according to one dated estimate from the New York Times.

What's more, I believe excessive internetting divides and might someday conquer us. In fact, it already spoils teamwork and our ability to have intelligent conversations about controversial topics, such as climate change, immunizations, nutrition, and politics. It does this because the unlimited amount of information and opinion found online actually heightens our susceptibility to confirmation bias, the cognitive disorder that most of us suffer from in which we tend to only listen to information that confirms our preconceptions and worldview rather than challenging us toward progress, compromise, and trade-offs.

Put simply, it increases hive-mindedness and groupthink.

Further, excessive internetting increases our susceptibility to information bias and the ostrich effect. The former has proven to weaken our decision-making since access to less information often results in more accurate predictions and decisions. The latter relates to the above. Since we can indulge and decide which worldview we choose to see now by filtering out things we don't like to confront, it's easier now to delude and shield ourselves from complex and uncomfortable realities. Thus, excessive internetting solidifies cognitive dissonance.

Make no mistake: I'm no conspiracy theorist. In no way was our current condition deliberately designed, evilly motivated, or put in place by anyone or any group in particular. It's really just shortsighted thinking and a lack of planning—the early stages and growing pains of the wild, wild, "digital West."

Nevertheless, our exposure to this brave new world has gone too far, especially among the sizable amount of the more compulsive ones among us. While there can never be too much information, we've learned the hard way that you can consume too much of it.

All told, excessive internetting is crippling our society, and so much so that I don't believe the Renaissance would have happened (or could happen again) with the amount of human distraction taking place now. Significant creative movements and cultural advancements demand far more attention and focus than our current society is able to give.

Of course, we're still capable of political unrest. We still get angry when we see injustice. And we're still exploring exciting opportunities such as privatized space travel, driverless cars, and prolonged human life. But, in most cases, we're too myopic, distant, or both to give a damn about more important things.

As an ironic advertisement from Apple recently asserted, "We've started to confuse convenience for joy, abundance for choice."

The company was talking about good smartphone design. But they may have well introduced a modern metaphor for the life created from overused internetting.

Chapter 7: Confirming his death

When I was younger and dumber, I used to work eleven-hour weekdays and half-day Saturdays, and I was mentally consumed with work for much of the remainder. Although I'm self-employed and enjoy a ridiculously flexible schedule, I vacationed very little back then. Like many twentysomethings, I was seeking fortune and fame, and I thought working more than sixty hours per week would get me there faster.

It didn't. Looking back, my previous overwork made me counterproductive, shortsighted, and less money on a per hour basis. In fact, Henry Ford discovered this a century ago, according to *Inc Magazine*.

As the story goes, Ford Motor Company ran dozens of tests in the early 1900s (what we now call "analytics") to determine the optimum number of work hours to achieve maximum productivity. In doing so, Ford discovered that the sweet spot for redundant assembly-line work was around thirty-five to forty hours per worker per week. He also learned that holding hours to sixty per week provided a temporary boost to productivity (20 percent more for three to four weeks only), after which productivity on sixty hours per week actually dropped to 50 percent of a normal forty hours per week.

Unsurprisingly, most workaholics would react to Ford's findings by thinking the rules don't apply to them, that history won't repeat itself, that times have changed, or that they'll be able to shun their bad habits later on because changing behavior is easy to do (it's not). Because of this, many will continue to repeat the same workaholic mistakes that Americans largely have committed since the '80s, the same decade in which the term "work-life balance" was coined.

More recently, new research from Stanford University suggests that twenty hours per week is ideal to maximize the creative, or non-assembly, output produced by writers, scientists, artists, and anyone else who wrangles their noggin in search of original output. "Decades of research demonstrate that the correlation between the number of hours worked and productivity is very weak," the researchers found. In fact, both Charles Dickens and Charles Darwin worked around twenty hours per week to achieve their similar levels of proficiency and influence. Old-school slackers, if you will.

Besides that, we're doing more in fewer hours, studies show. "Researchers note that productivity rates have risen, which theoretically lets many people be just as comfortable as previous generations while working less," reports the *New York Times*. Even visionaries admit as much. "The idea that everyone needs to work frantically is just not true," says former Google CEO Larry Page.

So workaholics must ask themselves, "Are you smarter than the past?" Or at least, "Do you have convincing and measurable evidence that overwork results in greater productivity?"

But that's not a fair question since we already know the answer. What we do know is this: many devout workaholics die alone—either literally or figuratively with strained relationships—and in poor health since they didn't work on their bodies as much as they worked on their careers. Many of them die with regret because they lived someone else's dream instead of their own or deferred more important priorities, such as health and loved ones, until it was too late.

Of all the research I've reviewed over the last decade, the Four Burners Theory is the leading explanation for the above common tragedy. The theory argues that an individual's life can be divided into four quadrants, or "burners," of a conventional stove: family, friends, health, and work. "In order to be successful you have to cut off one of your burners," the theory states. "And in order to be really successful you have to cut off two."

Which explains why iconic individuals—most recently Steve Jobs—often (if not always) sacrifice their relationships and personal health in pursuit of unmatched professional greatness. Conversely, it forces each of us to ask ourselves what we're willing to sacrifice in pursuit of our own notoriety. In most reported cases, greatness cannot be achieved with heat emanating from all four burners. But a meaningful and even exceptional life certainly can.

So the first step to living large and winning work on low-caloric technology is accepting the fact that humans—you, me, we, even superhuman ones—maximize their weekly productivity at around forty hours per week for rote workers and twenty hours for creative ones. That in itself is empowering because it allows each of us to be extremely precise and surgical in how we spend and prioritize our finite amounts of, not only work, but, ultimately, time spent awake.

In all cases, that means drastic distraction removal. In my case, that means rigging my smartphone to natively behave like a "dumb" device until I specifically ask it to get smart with me. That means no alerts, notifications, beeps, or buzzes of any kind save for voice calls, which is how all emergencies are still communicated. Furthermore, I don't see or hear text messages or emails until I decide it's time to check or unless they're from my wife. I'm also off all public social networking platforms save for one. And even for that one, I removed the app from my phone and only check it once or twice a week on my desktop while at work for promotional reasons.

As already mentioned, canceling my mobile internet for several years until I was finally capable of managing my own compulsions toward anytime internetting was another drastic measure I took. Noting that each person's challenges will be different, the important thing is to remove distractions that aren't significantly meaningful to your four burners. How do you know what's significantly meaningful to those? Do without the suspected distraction for a week, month, or year and see how it affects your productivity, relationships, and bottom line. From experience, my guess would be little to no effect whatsoever.

In fact, the moment I flipped the "no more distraction" switch nearly eight years ago, my personal, love, and social life all took an upward bending trajectory that would make venture capitalists green with envy.

And although seemingly counterintuitive, my professional life did the same—an equally upward trajectory. Self-absorbed workaholics won't believe me. I know the feeling; I used to be one. But after adopting alert-free and dumb-like phone and technology settings, I've largely enjoyed consecutive years of record income, social encounters, and sustained health ever since. Even better, my thousandaire coffers and social experiences are still trending upward. With few distractions, I'm better able to concentrate my focus, creativity, and attention into all four burners for maximum output. I may not be great, but I undoubtedly feel like I'm firing on all four burners and feel in complete control of my time, my commitments, and my ability to satisfy them all.

Admittedly, not everyone has the same psychological wiring as I do. And I don't presume to speak for every working professional, although I think my life-hacks apply to most white-collar workers, including many executives and entrepreneurs.

Consequently, your alert-free mileage will vary. But millions (if not billions globally) are susceptible to the same kinds of unhealthy behavior as I am. Pavlov proved this with his popular dog experiment, which explains why unexpected alerts or "rewards" of the internet and smartphones lead many of us to compulsion disorders and offline imbalance—which is why I wrote this book.

After recognizing our limits and setting boundaries on distractions, the next step is to identify, understand, and refrain from the most common temptations associated with overwork. They are as follows:

1. **Thinking we're "important" by working long hours.** People want their lives to have meaning. They don't want a third of it (i.e., the ideal time spent working) to be spent in vain. So we delude ourselves into thinking that our work has some cosmic purpose to justify working more hours, which, on the surface, would suggest more importance. But quantity is not the same as quality. If I'm really being honest, my epitaph should read: "Occupation: Helped companies sell more widgets and advertising with written words." None of us are *that* big of a deal. Yes, industry and economy are an important endeavor. But it's not as important as sharing a smile with someone, realizing your child will be smarter than you, feeling insignificant amid a majestic landscape, experiencing and nurturing true love, finding your groove, watching an underdog upset the establishment, catching a wave, or eating a homemade chocolate chip cookie. The sooner we accept our dispensability and nothingness, the sooner we'll rightfully fill our lives with greater, more qualitative meaning.

2. **Counting dollars and hours instead of fulfillment.** Humans like to keep score, get ahead, and one-up the Joneses. And one of the easiest ways to do that now is out-scheduling, staying busy, or working more than *they* do. In other words, measuring happiness and leisure is harder to do. So we measure hours worked, events scheduled, money accumulated, or even the misguided places visited instead. In doing so, we remain firmly on the gerbil wheel.

3. **Confusing busyness with productivity.** Have you ever wondered why some people bandy on about how busy they are? "I'm so busy!" they exclaim. "I don't even sleep!" They do this à la George Costanza, because they're inconsiderate of others (see also: tinyurl.com/neverbusy). And similar to reason number one, they're attempting to inject meaning into the otherwise trivial choices they make. Again, staying busy is easier than finding and undertaking fulfilling work. It's why we stay late at the office after a full day of wasted productivity. It's why we're incapable of leaving the office early, even though it's obvious our minds need a break. It's how we further lie to ourselves about the "work" we do.

4. **Succumbing to narcissism and being one-dimensional.** Ideally, people work eight hours, sleep eight hours, and split the rest of their day between varying degrees of hobbies, pastimes, way too much TV, and other personal choices (a.k.a. "leisure"). Next to sleep, many of us will spend more time doing one job than anything else, so we naturally identify more with that one thing than with anything else. Some of us even let that one thing wholly identify us. When that happens, we naturally spend more time doing that one thing because it's what we're most familiar and comfortable doing. That's how people become one-dimensional. It's how we become boring, uncultured, self-centered, and incapable of carrying on a conversation beyond work. It's why many of us overwork because it's the only thing we feel we're good at and valued for.

5. **Embracing the familiar instead of the extraordinary.** A hard work ethic is a wonderful thing, and Americans undeniably have that. We're also optimistic and hopeful. But we could be more confident about a reduced workweek and start working smarter instead of just longer. As respected economist John Maynard Keynes argued in his famous 1930 essay, which predicted our inability to take advantage of abundant leisure, "We have been trained too long to strive and not to enjoy."

But old dogs can learn new tricks. We can break the cycle of overwork. To accomplish this, however, each of us needs healthy amounts of hope, discipline, and accountability. We also need the Rule Of Thirds.

Chapter 8: Living large on low-caloric technology

In order to achieve balance, all of us must adopt the Rule Of Thirds. It works like this. Similar to separating our areas of focus into four functions, or "burners," the Rule Of Thirds divides our days into three activity buckets that deserve equal amounts of time and attention: sleep time (eight hours), work time (eight hours), and free time (eight hours). Here's a handy explanation of each:

Sleep time

Think of this like grabbing for your own oxygen mask in the event of an aeronautical emergency before helping other "passengers." Specifically, sleep time includes around eight hours of sleep for adults—give or take an hour each way, depending on the individual.

Numeral wizards will quickly note this isn't perfect math. But the Rule Of Thirds largely keeps to around eight hours per activity per day. That said, seven to eight hours of sleep applies to a whopping 99 percent of the population. In fact, only 1 percent of humans can sustainably live on four to six hours per night (a.k.a. "short sleepers"). Nevertheless, more than a third of Americans are sleep-deprived, reports Gallup. This is double what it was in 1942.

To put it simply, you are *not* the exception. You are the rule. So allocate seven to eight hours of sleep per night. Doing so will improve your appetite, immune system, memory, overall health, and lower the risk of disease, research shows. "For many people, getting sufficient sleep is increasingly under assault," writes Julia Kirby for Harvard Business Review. "In the three-legged stool of good health, nutrition and exercise are constantly discussed, while sleep has so far come up short."

To help achieve a healthy night's sleep, avoid stimulants (including caffeine, chocolate, nicotine, and alcohol); stick to a rigid sleeping routine; remove stress, distractions, light, and heat from your bedroom; and lastly—commit to regular exercise. I realize that's a lot to take in, so just start with good sleep if you must and slowly incorporate the rest.

In short, if you can master sleep time, it's much easier to balance the remaining two thirds. Which brings us to:

Work time

This primarily encompasses both occupational and fitness-related work, but it also includes tasks such as personal hygiene, housekeeping, bathroom breaks, groceries, required (not leisurely) shopping, car maintenance, grooming, part-time volunteering, and any other work you must do to sustain your and your family's way of life.

As for occupational time, stick to the above twenty to forty hours per week, depending on occupational type. In most cases, this occurs on weekdays. For regular exercise, commit to sixty to ninety minutes per week of vigorous, sweat-inducing, and exhausting heart and muscle work—the recommended amount, according to Mayo Clinic.

On top of that, your innards will require an additional amount of "moderate aerobic exercise," such as walking, recreational playtime, or mowing the lawn. As a general goal, aim for at least thirty minutes of physical activity per day, doctors say. That includes both vigorous and moderate activity. In my case, I engage in twenty minutes of vigorous exercise per weekday and more moderate exercise on nights and weekends while goofing off and tending to household and personal duties.

From there, you can use weekends to make up for any deficient work or delinquent exercise. Basically, you should earmark the remaining time for household items and personal to-dos. But you can't use all of your weekend (and neither your nights) for work-, exercise-, and maintenance-related stuff. We still have one more bucket that, like sleep, is often neglected but just as important.

Free time

The most complex and fluid of any third, this important column includes meals, recreation, leisure, adventure, relaxation (a.k.a. "downtime"), short napping not associated with sleep deprivation, entertainment, reading, screen time, music, spirituality, meditation, travel, and ideally lots of socializing with family and friends. All told, free time is what we commonly refer to as "the good things in life."

In my view, no sleep or work of any kind should be done in this block, at least not indefinitely or for extended periods of time. Granted, a sleep or work emergency can justifiably happen here. But only under extreme situations, such as after running a marathon or when thousands of dollars or someone's health is at stake. Given that, I don't think there's any reason to allocate more than two to three emergencies of either kind per year here. Most emergencies are imagined. So be extra careful when making exceptions to this.

57

In addition to letting your mind wander, the best use of free time is probably found in nutrition. Like the French and other seasoned cultures have long since figured out, meals are a social event—not a refueling pit stop, as many Americans treat them. The more time, care, and attention we give to our meals, the healthier we'll eat. It's why from-scratch cooking is so healthy for us, because fast food, preprepared desserts, and sugar water are more easily and quickly consumed.

While entertainment and relaxation are both important, so is perpetual education. I say that because formal education is usually finite. So our free time should also be filled with asking lots of good questions and pursuing the most proven or convincing answers with reliable sources, regular research, and critical thinking.

In addition to being the most fun of any column, free time is arguably where and when we grow the most as intellectual, emotional, and spiritual beings. It's often where we find the greatest amount of inspiration to fuel our work time and future free time.

Admittedly, for homemakers, single parents with dependent children, and indebted or impoverished people, this bucket often and understandably goes neglected. But it can and should be at least partially completed with sacrifices. Just make sure you sacrifice equally across personal, work, and free time, and then make up the difference on nights and weekends where you can.

In my family's case, that means extra relaxation on the weekends or one parent granting the other extra free time on nights as needed. Like sleep, free time is where you can and should take care of your own oxygen mask and mental well-being before helping others in the event of an emergency.

Looking back, I rarely lived the Rule Of Thirds for the first thirty years of my life. But for the last decade, I largely have, making it the greatest decade of my life so far.

Truth be told, a lot of people I encounter are surprised by my low-tech and fewer work hours lifestyle, mostly because the unstated mainstream view incorrectly assumes that staying on an internet-connected smartphone for extended periods and working overtime allows us to get ahead in life. It doesn't. It's just an illusion. In fact, all-day working and internetting actually lead to less inspired work, as both century-old and recent research both confirm.

Oddly, most people welcome additional work and tech into their lives unchecked, reports the *New York Times*. Why? Since we don't actually work more than we used to, according to decades of research conducted by John Robinson, the only answer is we've simply confused busyness as important work and shiny technology as significant. Therefore, we fill our free time with these mostly meaningless things and neglect our sleep and work time as a result—even though doing so prevents us from recharging our batteries and tackling tomorrow with hungrier and more motivated minds.

In summary, to kill the king and thrive on low-caloric technology, we must:

1. Respect our scientifically proven limits and recent productivity gains.
2. Remove distractions that add to our workload without boosting our output.
3. Understand the most common temptations associated with overwork and indulgent technology use.
4. Separate and spend equal amounts of our day on sleep, work (professional and personal), and free time.
5. Treat food (a.k.a. three meals a day) as an event to be savored rather than a pit stop or quick refueling trip.

6. Ask "Why?" instead of "Why not?" (and have a good answer for the former) when taking on new work and technology commitments.

For more helpful tips, please read tinyurl.com/ top10health.

Chapter 9: The power of feeling "forever alone"

The inability to be alone in thought is the biggest down-side of excessive internetting and never-ending busy-ness. If we truly believe that the mind is a powerful thing, why would we willingly inundate, interrupt, or regularly waste it with ceaseless digital noise?

In search of a few timely laughs, comedian Louis C.K. may have found the answer. "I think these things are toxic," he said of so-called "smartphones." He went on to describe peculiar behaviors we're all familiar with: head down, failing to look people in the eye, and suffer-ing anxiety, loneliness, or even temporary sadness when we find ourselves without company.

To avoid these uncomfortable but natural feelings, "we break out our phones," C.K. says. It's so bad that "people are willing to take a life and risk their own while texting and driving, because they don't want to be alone for a second."

That's what smartphones have taken away. "The ability to just sit there, to be yourself, and not be doing something. The ability to be completely sad or com-pletely happy."

Heavy stuff—doubly so from a morally compro-mised comedian.

Why do we behave this way? Because we're unwilling or uncomfortable confronting our own feelings now, especially loneliness. When we do that, we bypass the inherent motivation needed to ultimately find sustained fulfillment, meaning, and purpose in life. In doing so, we willingly numb ourselves, not with digital drugs or "Soma," as previously mentioned from Huxley's scarily accurate Brave New World, but with nonstop distractions of which there are a bottomless amount of online.

Nevertheless, an old black and white photo recently went viral after being shared online by technocrats. The caption read: "All this technology is making us anti-social." The photo was taken at the back of passenger train and depicted thirty to forty commuters, almost all of which were reading newspapers instead of romantically conversing with and learning from one another.

Although cute and funny, the photo does not absolve excessive internet use. It may rightfully prove that humans have always kept their heads down, at least when traveling on public transportation. But eventually those same humans looked up. Newspapers and books have a final page, after all. The internet doesn't. Which puts us in a worse position today for confronting our feelings, fears, and triumphs than before.

Yes, there have always been distractions in life, and there always will be. But the unending levels achieved by the internet, social media, millions of apps, streaming entertainment, and twenty-four-hour "news" are a force to be reckoned with. And so far, humans aren't reckoning very well.

Because of this, we never feel completely sad or completely happy. Which is probably why you've chosen to read this far.

Simple awareness, it turns out, is the best way to counter this feeling. So we must remove the biggest distraction of all from our life if we want that awareness to happen. For many of us, bottomless internet, social media, and busy work is our biggest distraction.

As writer extraordinaire David Foster Wallace once taught in his renowned commencement speech at Kenyon College, "The most obvious realities are hardest to see and talk about." Why? Because rather than confront "the essential lonesomeness of adult life," he said, most of us avoid rather than savor the "boredom, routine, and petty frustration" associated with adult life.

"If you're automatically sure that you know what reality is, and you are operating on your default setting, then you, like me, probably won't consider possibilities that aren't annoying and miserable. But if you really learn how to pay attention, then you will know there are other options."

The other options include embracing the moment—even tedious and meaningless ones—rather than giving in to the misguided and irrational "fear of missing out." Instead of being elsewhere in thought, picking up our phones, living vicariously online, or avoiding an often monotonous present moment, we can decide what has meaning. "That is freedom," Wallace emphasized. "The alternative is the rat race."

Admittedly, "It is unimaginably hard to do this—to stay conscious and alive in the adult world day after day, week after week, month after month, year after year," he concluded. Which is why excessive online use affects so many of us. But "it will actually be within your power to experience a crowded, hot, slow, consumer-hell type situation as not only meaningful, but sacred—on fire with the same force that made the stars."

A little over the top? Maybe. But sage advice and the world's greatest thinkers (see: tinyurl.com/greatest-thinkers) all agree: living in the reality that's placed in front of us is always a more worthwhile existence than nostalgically living in the past or unceasingly living in the future, that latter of which should not be confused with goal-setting. There's a difference between setting goals and worshipping them. The former is healthy. The latter is debilitating.

Deep down, I suspect the collective internet already knows this. In recent years, the phrase "forever alone" was coined, shared, and meme-ified countless times online. What does it even mean? It means the same thing that the world's greatest philosophers often talk about. As social creatures, we all share a deep-rooted fear of being alone. Which is why we're so terrified of death. It doesn't get any more alone than ceasing to exist, possibly forever.

To avoid that unbearable possibility, many of us try to distract ourselves with as many pleasures and busyness as we can get our hands on. We've done this since the dawn of time. But as mentioned in chapter 2, the modern internet affords each of us with more distractions, instant gratification, and perceived power than the world's greatest kings ever had access to. And no one gives power up that easily.

But good kings don't rule for power. They rule for self and collective wellness. You can be one of those kings. You can willingly forgo the perceived and illusionary power of excessive internetting, digital relationships, and overwork by removing him or her from power.

How can this be done? First, be conscious of how and when you engage the internet, social media, and work. In my case, I accept that all three things have improved my life. Not only do they make me more productive, social, informed, and empowered, they've indexed and revealed the world in a way that was previously unavailable to any of us. Nevertheless, I try to only reach for them now with purpose and meaning.

For example, unless there's legitimate and urgent business to attend to, I do not pull out my mobile fun box at dinner tables, in waiting lobbies, doctors' offices, or while in the presence of my kids, wife, or friends. When in public, I make it a point never to use my phone as a social anxiety blanket.

When alone and facing boredom, I may reach for the internet to socialize with distant friends. But in these moments, I prefer to use it for live voice calls or to schedule a future encounter because, as social creatures, digital relationships aren't nearly as rewarding, memorable, and fulfilling as in-person ones. With those kinds of relationships, you never feel completely sad or completely happy. So we must use these powerful devices to increase the number of in-person meetings we enjoy rather than to supplant them with.

To borrow a phrase from Wallace, the "capital T truth" is that we cannot find fulfillment with our heads down. And mobile internet, social media, and digital work undeniably keep our heads down significantly more than any other distraction or legitimate medium ever has before. If you're going to make meaningful connections to people, you must look at them and the life in front of us directly in the eye.

To experience the full range of emotion we as sentient beings were either meant or accidentally engineered to experience, we must be aware. We must face the possibility of loneliness. We cannot do this as cowardly, lazy, and insecure kings.

Despite how weak it sounds, I truly believe that keeping our phones in our pockets is one of the bravest things any of us can do.

Chapter 10: Taking action; finding your flow

Although initially apprehensive about my weeklong, life-changing trip to Montana—"How am I supposed to continue my affair with work and feed my fear of missing out without the internet being there!?"—I was changed by it within a matter of days. Again, with no online distractions, the social aspect had dramatically improved.

Heads were no longer dropping to their laps every few minutes. Robotic acknowledgments that a point had been made were a thing of the past. Smartphone orphans had their parents back. Minds were no longer distracted with what was happening elsewhere. As a group, we were living in the moment, à la *Little House on the Prairie*, only with much nicer amenities. It was the most eye-opening and worthwhile vacation I have ever been on.

The week after my "Montana Moment," I decided this was how I wanted to live for the rest of my life. I still wanted to use technology, mobile computing, and the internet to my professional and personal advantage. But I also wanted to put it down on nights and weekends, as if it were a briefcase being dropped by the front door upon returning home. Since then, I've done just that.

"But times have changed, man," many have told me in disbelief. "You can't live like that now. You have to be connected all the time if you want to get ahead, especially for an online guy like you." Nearly a decade later, I can honestly say: "No, you don't." If you are feeling burned out, overwhelmed, stuck in a perpetual rut of screen refreshes, new message checks, gadget obsessions, or status updates, there is another way.

I call it Reformed Luddism, and I'd encourage you to consider it. It's not nearly as radical or knee-jerk as the original industrial Luddites from the nineteenth century, whom I refer to as the original gangsters of anti-technology. In fact, to be a Reformed Luddite, all you have to do is recognize the many benefits of personal technology but do so with an untrusting eye. Then only accept the ones that are relevant to your season in life and are easily manageable.

For example, instead of joining the new rat race, the Reformed Luddite rejects the notion of keeping up with the Joneses, the geeks, the hipsters, or workaholics. They're slow to adopt and resist the latest software and hardware until proven useful *to them* specifically. They're acutely aware of the unanticipated consequences of new media. They are quick to abandon the binary ones and zeros that no longer work for them and seek out tools that actually save time as opposed to demanding more of it.

In short, the Reformed Luddite prefers a low-caloric digital diet and is picky about what he or she consumes. If they don't love the considered technology or innovation, they expunge it from their lives—if not temporarily until it is improved, they do so permanently. The Reformed Luddite still appreciates the conveniences of the information age, namely Google Maps and speakers named Alexa that they can bark commands at for quick information. But they favor analog, offline experiences more. They rightfully distinguish simulated life from authentic life, and they recognize the importance of both while striving for the latter.

And that's what this book is really all about—to be a voice of reason amid all this wonderful but mostly use-less, fleeting, noisy stuff. The stuff that really doesn't matter. The stuff that gets in the way of a trip to Big Sky Country, imagination, awareness, good conversation, intimacy, focus, impermanence, love, loneliness, full range of feeling, and individual determination.

Eight years after first embracing the Reformed Luddite movement, I can confidently say I'm better off than I was before. I probably won't see that popular cat video as fast as you. I certainly won't know what *Star Wars* character my friends would be after taking a dopey online quiz. But it's liberating to be able to say, "It can wait until tomorrow or Monday. I'm having too much fun right now to worry about that."

In light of all of this, I suspect you're probably feel-ing similar apprehension as I did about pulling in the digital reins. You might even feel overwhelmed. The good news is there's lots of help. And I'm going to share everything I've encountered, researched, interviewed, studied, and discovered on my ten-year journey for do-ing just that:

Intervene

First, we need to diagnose your "condition" and/or any disorder you may be suffering from. To do that, I recommend starting with the Internet Addiction Diag-nostic Questionnaire (quoted below). If you honestly answer "yes" to at least five of the below, you probably have an internet compulsion disorder according to the latest medical advice:

1. Do you feel preoccupied with the internet (i.e., think about previous online activity or anticipate your next online session)?
2. Do you feel the need to use the internet with increas-ing amounts of time in order to achieve satisfaction?

3. Have you repeatedly made unsuccessful efforts to control, cut back, or stop internet use?
4. Do you feel restless, moody, depressed, or irritable when attempting to cut down or stop internet use?
5. Do you stay online longer than originally intended?
6. Have you jeopardized or risked the loss of significant relationship, job, educational or career opportunities because of the internet?
7. Have you lied to family members, therapists, or others to conceal the extent of involvement with the internet?
8. Do you use the internet as a way of escaping from problems or of relieving a dysphoric mood (e.g., feelings of helplessness, guilt, loneliness, anxiety, or depression)?

In my case, I answered yes to questions one, two, three, five, six, seven, and eight. Whatever your response, admitting that there is, or may be, a problem is the first step toward improvement. If you need a more objective, less biased evaluation, consider enlisting the help of a trusted friend, family, or confidant before answering the above.

Understand

For many of us, excessive internetting is just a really bad habit—the digital equivalent of sucking our thumb, biting our nails, overeating, overspending, smoking, or abusing other addictive substances. When succumbing to this and other bad habits, we create a new normal that is anything but. Which explains why so many of us feel more comfortable online than offline now.

How is that possible? "Our brains are sensitive to stimuli, and if you spend a lot of time with a particular mental experience or stimulus, the neural circuits that control that mental experience will strengthen," reports neuroscientist Gary Small, a brain researcher at UCLA. "At the same time, if we neglect certain experiences, the circuits that control those will weaken."

In other words, if we're not having real-time conversations or looking people in the eye (i.e., basic human contact skills), those skills will weaken, Small says. In that sense, digital relationships, too much asynchronous communication, and social media that doesn't result in actual social encounters are one giant mirage.

Not only that, but it increases feelings of detachment, doctors observe. To counter this isolated feeling, many of us try to remedy it with a greater number of hastily answered interruptions such as status updates, messages, app alerts, and email that overload our dopamine system and cause a frustrating feedback loop —that horrible rut you feel when you keep checking and checking without anything ever happening.

There is good news, however, if not light at the end of the tunnel. While the majority of people (an estimated 70 percent) check their phones within an hour of waking up or going to bed, and a similar number do so constantly on weekends and vacation, people who refrain from doing so are twice as happy as those who succumb to the modern human default setting and digital rat race. Leslie Perlow, a Harvard Business School professor and author of *Sleeping with Your Smartphone*, found that 78 percent of those who disconnected from work at night reported satisfaction with their jobs, while only 49 percent of those who used their smartphones at night reported the same level of satisfaction.

That is to say, patience is a must when striving for offline balance. This is because people don't change very much or very fast. They can certainly change—they regularly do—and many have. But don't be dismayed when you fall off the wagon. Reset your sights and cele- brate the progress you have made while striving for greater offline balance.

Take action

If you're one of the many who compulsively checks your smartphone, there are several ways to overcome this. Three big ones are as follows:

1. **Be conscious.** Identify and understand your feelings before picking up your phone. For example, are your phone, internet, or work compulsions triggered by boredom? Loneliness? Anxiety? Fear of missing out? Whatever it is, make a note of it and try to process this feeling rather than suppressing or avoiding it with infinite internetting or overwork. Additionally, check your motive before sharing something online. Is it to show off, project something, to mask an insecurity you have, or is it to genuinely enrich your personal, professional, and other social relationships?

2. **Be disciplined.** More specifically, turn off all alerts. Disable every audible and visual notification unless it's coming from your spouse, children, boss or other V.I.P. I cannot stress this enough. It will take work, however, since most apps default to notifications. Moving forward, always reject notifications. Never let apps or your phone disturb you. Go to them when you find yourself in need rather than letting them interrupt your day. This sucks, I know, especially since newspapers and old-school electronics didn't say, "Hey, pick me up!" But modern devices do. Don't let them unless it's an emergency or from the most important people in your life. Willpower alone is not enough, and there is no other way: you must disable virtually all alerts and notifications.

3. **Set usage boundaries.** From today on, you'll need to decide ahead of time how and when you will use your phone in certain situations. For instance, will you reach for it when you're with your children, spouse, or friends, or while driving, eating, or in a meeting—or at a funeral? In addition to specific circumstances, what times will you knowingly stay off it? Between 9 p.m. and 7 a.m. perhaps? Will you take it to bed? Will you enable "do not disturb" mode during sleep? How will you reach for your phone on weekends and vacation? Whatever you decide, know that the stricter you are with your boundaries, the more satisfied, liberated, and balanced you'll be offline. Lastly, you'll need to limit your apps and treat them as guilty until proven innocent. Add nothing unless it has a specific and meaningful use to you. And when adding something, always consider removing an app you rarely or no longer use. After all, the more apps you allow into your life, the more mental baggage you carry. The worst that could happen is you can always redownload a deleted app later if you really miss it that much.

In some cases, however, you may be forced to completely remove the connected distraction. When asked what kind of therapy or treatment should be prescribed for someone who feels out of control online, or is otherwise neglecting their offline life, the aforementioned Dr. Weinschenk told me: "You've got to break the dopamine loop and go offline completely to stop the triggers and cues that information is coming in. To reset your expectation of offline interactions, it often requires going cold turkey online."

It certainly did for me. In fact, I canceled mobile data for three whole years before reintroducing it into my life. Yes, it was a pain to print driving directions beforehand like we used to do at the turn of the twenty-first century. But rewiring my brain to a new offline normal was entirely worth it.

Even to this day, my family and I continue to take offline sabbaticals once or twice a year for an entire week, as mentioned previously. No electronics, no phones, no TV, no movies, no internet (save for work), no social media, no anything media. Nuthin'. Doing this helps us cultivate and rediscover our offline passions while reminding us of and emphasizing the online media we miss and enjoy most so we can prioritize it after returning from sabbatical.

In an effort to regain control of their lives, some people—including comedian Aziz Ansari—permanently lobotomize their phones. To do this, they remove any web browser, email app, social media, and any other feature that offers an infinite amount of updates. Many keep only the camera, navigational maps, weather, and phone and messaging apps to stay in touch with close friends and family.

Others turn to dumb phones for old-school voice and text messaging, without the apps. Whatever you decide, correcting extreme internet use almost always requires extreme measures. To recalibrate your dopamine and offline awareness, you will need a sustained and prolonged (if not permanent) break from online things that are no longer of value. But you cannot determine which are of value with an often distorted view and use of these powerful tools. To do that, you must take a sustained break from them.

For those that do, however, I cannot describe the liberating amount of productivity, satisfaction, focus, and invigoration you'll discover after resetting your online life. And I assure you: it comes with all of the conveniences without any of the distractions and feelings of powerlessness. Simply put, it is a revelation I cannot wait for you to experience in your own time, on your own terms, and in your own way after following some or all of the above advice and guidance.

One final and important point: While some readers may be able to do this on their own, others will likely need the help and second opinion of a therapist or even doctor. Gauging your personal progress or lack thereof is the best way to know. In the event of the latter, you'll probably need outside help.

Chapter 11: Getting back online and winning life with no regrets

Unlike most behavioral changes in my life, I can pinpoint the exact moment I committed to and found offline balance: June of 2009. I cemented that change shortly thereafter upon canceling my mobile internet and deleting my Facebook account. (Spoiler alert: I still have friends.)

No going back, I thought at the time.

Which wasn't exactly true. Although I've largely remained "social-media free" since then, I reintroduced myself to mobile internet a few years later. I remember welcoming the added convenience it would bring, but I was also a little apprehensive about falling into bad habits again.

Thankfully, I didn't. In the proceeding years I lived with a WiFi-only smartphone, I was able to form new habits and boundaries that I have since maintained, namely conducting work and professional correspondence only on weekdays, turning off all electronic notifications save for my alarm clock and voice calls, never robbing myself of free time on nights, weekends, or vacations, and living in the moment for myself, my family, and friends closest to me.

Always the trooper, my wife supported me in this endeavor and even played along. A year after I quit Facebook, she followed suit and remained that way for many years. She also never complained about the several years we "endured" with no mobile internet.

Then Instagram happened and most of her friends pleaded with her to rejoin the digital fold. She came to me one day and announced she was "returning to social media." I was a little anxious about this, given all of the growth and good times we had enjoyed in the past six years. But I supported her and viewed it as an opportunity for her to cultivate more friendships, which I felt she needed as a full-time mother and homemaker.

At first after registering for her free account, she felt empowered, like many of us feel after joining trendy new social circles, digital or otherwise. She was having fun, rekindling old relationships, and forming new ones. I, too, was happy for her.

Then things started to sour. Instead of her giving me that disapproving look while cheating the present with an online quickie, I began giving her *that look*. We talked about it and set new boundaries, but I suspected she still wasn't happy. What started as a mechanism to enhance her social life had become an unnecessary distraction and constant source of consternation for her.

A year and a half later, she surprised me with the bold and courageous announcement to quit social media again. She's come full circle, and I can honestly say she seems happier, less distracted, and more focused than ever on the things that are important to her.

Why am I telling you this? Because finding, maintaining, and reestablishing offline balance is a lifelong pursuit, not a "one and done" occurrence. Even to this day, after nine years of mostly offline equilibrium, I still have to fend against digital uprisings and new sieges from aspiring "kings" attempting to attack my castle. Like regular fitness or healthy eating, achieving offline bliss is a lifelong endeavor. Here are some behaviors to help you do that.

You got me offline—now what?

By the time I reined in my internet use, I was large-ly dependent on it for news, videos, communication, games, scheduling, socializing, research, and all manner of work and hobbies. Leaving it left a large void that was difficult to fill at first.

Perhaps you feel the same. If so, here's what you can do about it:

1. **Commit to working less.** If you don't have a plan, many people will likely resort to the default behavior of working more to fill the void. As the second great-est regret of the dying, working more will not make you happier, according to researcher Bronnie Ware. On the contrary, working less can actually increase the quality of your work while maintaining, if not im-proving, your output. As the forward-thinking Jason Fried once explained, "Constraining time encourages quality time. When you have a compressed work-week, you focus on what's important."

2. **Reach for hobbies that don't involve your phone.** If you enjoy games, consider playing them on a dedi-cated game console or handheld instead. If you enjoy reading, consider paperbacks, or at least a Kindle that doesn't have additional distracting apps. If you enjoy socializing, plan a party, lunch, dinner, or outing with friends or people you'd like to know better. Whatever you do, opt for things that don't involve your phone or overreliance on the internet.

3. **Cultivate former and new hobbies.** Did you used to kayak or play team sports? Maybe you used to hike or work in the garage with your hands more? Whatev-er it is, or whatever you've dreamed of doing, consider doing it anew or trying it for the first time. By all means, use the internet to research your hobbies. But don't live a simulated version of them online. Do them *in person*.

4. **Put your subconscious to work.** Early in my career, I read dozens of business and personal development books. While two or three stick out, I've largely forgotten the rest. Why? Because many of them repeat the same things. In fact, I've found much more professional and personal inspiration reading classics such as *Tom Sawyer*, *Frankenstein*, and *The Count of Monte Cristo* than I ever did while reading books like mine that spell everything out for the reader. This is because the former do a better job than the latter in letting our subconscious do the heavy lifting, something that scientific research proves we can only do if we give our mind the chance to concentrate on seemingly unrelated mental activities.

5. **Establish expectations with important relationships.** That goes for bosses, clients, coworkers, friends, and family. Doing so is not only courteous to them, but it will help you be responsive without being on the internet all the time. In my case, that means never answering an email on nights, weekends, or on vacation, even if I want to. It requires patience, but you'd be amazed at how little email I get during off-hours. This wasn't the case when I used to answer at all hours. Your behavior here will largely determine your own positive experiences.

6. **Explore the world around you more.** That might mean planning, anticipating, and taking long-distance trips you've always wanted to do. But it could also mean dorking around in your own backyard or people-watching in your own downtown. The more you explore the real-world around you, the more you'll appreciate, learn, and be drawn to it.

7. **"Retire" several times a year instead of once in a lifetime.** This works extremely well but requires a change of definition in what retiring and vacationing mean. In my case, they both mean short, quarterly breaks that may last four to five days over a long weekend. Doing this not only saves money and grants the benefits of time off today (rather than deferring it to the end of my life), but it lets my subconscious work and makes me hungrier and more motivated when I return to work and everyday life.

8. **Portion control your technology.** Don't call it a diet —by this I mean reducing your app, news, feeds, social networks, information, insipid subscriptions, unfiltered distractions in your life, and time spent in front of glowing objects. As part of that, consider all apps and new technology as guilty until proven useful to you and your specific goals. The best way I know how to do this is by becoming a late adopter and embracing that mind-set over the default and distracting and stress-inducing mindset of an early adopter. That, and deleting all software accounts that you no longer use and only adding something to your life if you can remove a previous technology that doesn't work as well.

9. **Restrict your phone to make it smarter.** That means things like turning off all alerts and notifications, never taking your phone to bed, enabling "do not disturb" mode, limiting your apps, and valuing facetime over screen time among others (see also: tinyurl.com/8moretips). Additionally, "no news" doesn't mean you should go looking for it out of habitual boredom. Let news come to you—it always does.

10. **Sometimes the best move in life is to do nothing.**
Avid chess readers and *Tron: Legacy* fans will already appreciate this. When the pressure is on, sometimes the best move in life is not to play the game. Wait and let your subconscious mind and original thought come to you before forcing something. This is especially true when filling the void left behind after leaving large parts of the internet behind. So do nothing. Breathe. Relax. Change won't come overnight, but it will never come if you don't give yourself a chance to decide what you want to do with the new time, flexibility, and control you've reclaimed in your life after equalizing your internet usage.

A note on work-life blending

In recent years, a new ideology has emerged. It is this: work-life balance is impossible; therefore, humanity must embrace work-life blending instead.

I tried work-life blending for six years before we ever called it that. I'm here to tell you it stinks and is largely a pipe dream—nothing more than a new term coined by self-absorbed workaholics to justify their personal regrets, negligence, and imbalances in life.

Now let me tell you how I really feel.

The phrase *work-life balance* entered our lexicon when faxes reigned supreme, the 1980s. Knowledge workers, globalization, and computer networking went mainstream that decade, and, with it, the temptation to work 'round the clock on the Hedonic Treadmill (i.e., the misguided belief that the more money one makes, the happier they'll be).

In response, first-world countries had a real first-world problem on their hands. The more connected their workers felt to the office, the more pressure they felt to "get ahead" by staying on the clock for extended periods of time. With only twenty-four hours in a day, something had to give.

That something usually involved personal health—since knowledge workers lead sedentary lives—but also strained relationships, lack of spirituality, forsaken hobbies or leisure that excite and recharge the mind, continuing education, and an inability to carry on a conversation beyond work.

Today, the so-called "boundaryless workplace" has become exponentially worse. We check email first thing in the morning and last thing at night. Our professional inboxes and to-do lists alert us wherever we go, often intruding on our free time. Leading corporate perks even include in-office dry cleaning, fitness centers, and three gourmet meals a day, which tempt us to rub elbows with work associates even more, helping everyone else's bottom line at the expense of our own.

Enter work-life balance. Although poorly named—work is an important part of life, not a conflicting aspect of it—the term's intent is right on the money: to balance regular demands on our time, including work responsibilities, loving relationships, physical and mental well-being, and individual pursuits.

At some point, however—perhaps because we're so miserable at it—work-life balance became "work-life blending," or integration. Instead of confronting the reality that our relationship to work is often at odds with sleep time and free time (which includes family time), some of us have embraced a fictional, consequence-free environment where anything goes. There are no trade-offs for the decisions we make. With work-life blending, we don't have to sacrifice anything.

Of course, that's nonsense. If you're mentally at the office all the time, there will be consequences. Strained relationships, a shorter life, and one-dimensional thinking top the list. Do it for a lifetime, and you'll likely die alone, the aforementioned Ware found. Conversely, if you shirk work, you'll likely end up fired, unmarketable, low-qualified, outdated, or with no income, all of which depress life.

You see, the work-life discussion is really just proof that we can't have it all. Life involves trade-offs. Everything happens for a reason, according to a popular adage, and sometimes the reason is that we're stupid and we make bad decisions.

Call it what you will, but ambitious professionals will always be confronted with imbalance, discord, competing priorities, compromise, and conflicting responsibilities. How we manage the boundaries of life determines whether we find equilibrium or become self-absorbed, relationship-neglecting narcissists unable to live in the moment and look down at glowing objects instead of into people's' eyes when they speak to us.

The day I finally reconciled my professional ambitions with personal obligations was the day I drew up specific boundaries for work, family, friends, health, and leisure. "Make time" is a phrase we often hear. To do that, I populate and consult an integrated life calendar with work, personal, and family activities side by side— ones that are as important as they are required of me. If the last nine years are any indication, it's worked.

Since we're all different, there's no right way to lead a balanced, harmonious life. No silver bullet to overcome conflicting work and personal commitments.

Some people incessantly work because they only identify with what they contribute to the world: master gadget salesman (Steve Jobs), master physicist (Einstein), master composer (Mozart). Others enduringly work to provide for their families or to finance personal interests such as travel, amateur athletics, extreme adventure, or other passions.

And some do all of the above with just the right mix of passion and responsibility. You may not know them by name. But you can bet they have their sanity.

Never forget: the internet is wonderful

If you'll recall from chapter 4, I mentioned my first "internet pen pal" from Southampton, England. I often stayed up late speaking to this lad. As a suburb-living American, I was amazed that people in foreign lands rode their bikes as often as he did—all over town, really.

Classic naïveté, to be sure. But conversing with him was a wonderful and eye-opening experience for me made possible by the internet. I've since had many more wonderful and eye-opening experiences online, even moreso after my pivotal "Montana Moment." And I meant what I said in the prologue: I wouldn't be where I am today without the internet.

But our phones and the internet that magically powers them are much more wonderful when used in moderation. A balanced internet lets us do more in less time, improve our relationships with family, friends, and coworkers, and read, if not ultimately learn, more than is possible through updated, every-second "junk" information. When used in moderation, the internet lets us socialize more, increase the number of in-person encounters, and ultimately live larger and better.

That said, overthrowing and killing the king is hard to do. But one thing the last nine years have taught me is that it can certainly be done. And it's absolutely liberating on both professional and personal levels.

Either way, I wish you success.

Epilogue: What I hope you learned

Congratulations—you made it to the final chapter. As a final parting shot, and before sending you off into the great unknown, I'd like to summarize all the preceding bulleted points and words of wisdom.

But first, an important qualifier.

Obviously, there are many ways to find balance in life. That goes for professional, mental, moral, physical, spiritual, communal, entertainment, and social reasons. It also goes for striking a balance between your online and offline pursuits, two "life forms" that are increasingly intertwined as they are important. But I believe, from first-hand experience, that offline pursuits are more significant, and I feel strongly that most people would agree with me. Which is why we must individually and collectively be aware of, temper, and constantly adjust to the powerful pull of the internet.

To be clear, I do not consider myself *the* authority on this subject. But the many years of experimenting, learning, and achieving some semblance of success, empowerment, and satisfaction offline does make me someone worth listening to. After all, I'm not just throwing untested theories and ideas at you. This book is the result of nearly 10 years of work, personal experimentation, and corresponding research on the effect that excessive internetting has on human behavior.

Furthermore, there are undoubtedly areas of life you've probably mastered that I'm still working on. Maybe I can read your book on that. But since this is my book, I'm taking as many liberties as I'm allowed in sharing my story, advice, and encouragement. If you take only one lesson with you after reading this book, I hope it's the following: finding internet equilibrium is a lifelong challenge that each of us must be cognizant of and brave enough to face with disciplined and calculated use while gently encouraging those closest to us (if not each other) to do the same.

In greater detail, I hope you'll leave with a better understanding and strong consideration of the following:

1. Achieving a modern and optimized lifestyle isn't easy, but it's worth the effort.
2. Indulgent information and technology junkies can lead more fulfilling online, offline, professional, and personal lives after hitting reset on internet abuse.
3. Although small, the "offline balance movement" is real and justified.
4. Workaholic habits, self-absorption, and all-consuming identities have gotten worse in the information and mobile eras and are counterintuitively hindering our wealth, welfare, and inspiration.
5. Reform Luddism is the best-known way to combat technology indulgence.
6. Join the cause: register for my free monthly newsletter at blakesnow.com/logoff-newsletter to stay up to date. Unsubscribe with one click the moment it no longer works for you.
7. This message is worth spreading. Please consider buying and sharing a copy of this book with friends, family members, and/or coworkers in need. If money is tight, lend them this copy. (Bonus: if you feel you didn't get your money's worth after reading this book, please email your proof of purchase to inbox@blakesnow.com, and I'll gladly refund you.)

If you're strongly considering some (or all) of the preceding advice, I want to add that I believe you can do this. I probably don't know you personally. But that you've read even this far convinces me that you're capable of achieving it. I say this for two reasons: 1) The internet isn't going anywhere—you can always go back to it. And 2) Your phone and inbox will never run out on you.

Be warned, however: if you do decide to "rage against the machine" of default internetting and phone use, you'll quickly find yourself in the minority. After all, over 70 percent of Americans own a smartphone and use social media, according to Pew Research. And only 20 percent of employers have a formal policy regulating the use of wireless communication devices during non-work hours, reports *USA Today*. In other words, you will undoubtedly face some social blowback and peer pressure.

Pay no mind to this, or at least take it as a compliment that others want you included. Either way, take heart to what Nobel Prize winner Herbert Simon said way back in 1978: "A wealth of information creates a poverty of attention." The same is true of internetting, overwork, and smartphones.

In fact, multiple studies from respected American, British, German, and other international universities all conclude that social media makes us envious, hyper-distracted, and loudmouthed individuals. Similar reports from respected news publications estimate that our off-line imbalance is costing the U.S. economy billions. Statistically, our collective "dependence syndrome" is real and having a negative impact on society.

No, it's not the end of the world. I'm a firm believer that the vast majority of us live in the greatest era of human civilization by far. But we can make it even better after finding offline balance.

In short, the good life is a genuine, responsible, devoted, and active one. If you want to lead a happy, flourishing, and meaningful life, you must be true to yourself. Nearly every great thinker and most religions admonish this.

In opposite terms, the Hedonic Treadmill isn't authentic. It's insecure groupthink. And you can't be extraordinary, which postmodern philosophy argues gives meaning, while following the herd. So devote yourself to virtuous, mostly offline passions. Be persistent (see: tinyurl.com/BePersistent). Remember that the kite string and self-imposed limitations actually enable flight and buy us more precious time to fly even higher. Most of all, be the hero (not the villain) of your own autobiography, as German philosopher Friedrich Nietzsche famously taught. You cannot do this if you're always distracted with work, your smartphone, or what's happening elsewhere online.

Lastly, forgive yourself if you're not happy with who, what, or where you are. Then commit to bettering yourself. Always consider if what you're doing is moving you toward deeper, more enriching relationships or a monotonous, more passive existence. Abhor real-time information. It is mostly a lie. Know that the cream of life always rises to the top, and that you don't have to know or even hear about it while it's rising. In fact, you cannot fully enjoy or appreciate the cream until it's fully separated.

In that noble pursuit, I wish you more than luck.

Credits

My sincerest and deepest thanks to the giants in my life who made this book possible: my devoted and loving wife, Lindsey Snow, my five lively children, my confidence-boosting parents—Brent and Cathy Snow—my keeping-me-honest siblings, my supportive in-laws, my reassuring extended family, those who have generously paid me to write for them, and The Man Upstairs (or evolutionary good luck) for putting me and all these cool people, creatures, and plants on the only life-filled planet in the known universe.

I'd also like to thank early supporters of this book: my loyal blog readers, Susan Weinschenk, the many respected agents that passed on but encouraged this book, the numerous researchers and reporters cited herein, my editor, Blake Atwood, Amazon Publishing, and the many tough-love editors that previously taught me how to write well, namely Vlad Coho, Kristin Kalning, Sid Shuman, Erik Malinowski, Alan Alper, and anyone else who invested their own time to improve my writing with spelling, grammar, facts, and diction corrections (see also: tinyurl.com/dictionbad).

Additional shout-outs to my lifelong friends Josh Rhine and Wesley Lovvorn, Matt and Susan Andersen, the influential Jeremy Anderson, the forgiving front office manager from the Atlanta Hawks, The Ormond Brothers, Dustin Larsen, The Terry Family, Nick Wentzel, Oxford commas, and the many believing readers that stuck with me until completion of this book.

Thank you.

NOTE: If you finished this book, please consider reviewing it on Amazon.com. I also accept comments, rants, and raves at inbox@blakesnow.com and hope to find you on my website some day: blakesnow.com. Now, enjoy your life!

95276112R00063

Made in the USA
San Bernardino, CA
21 November 2018